The Other Life

Books by Herbert Scott

Sleeping Woman
Durations
Groceries
Disguises

The Other Life:
Selected Poems of Herbert Scott

Edited by David Dodd Lee

Carnegie Mellon University Press

Pittsburgh 2010

Acknowledgments

Poems herein have been selected from: *Disguises* (University of Pittsburgh Press, 1974), *Groceries* (University of Pittsburgh Press, 1976), *Durations* (Louisiana State University Press, 1984), and *Sleeping Woman* (Carnegie Mellon University Press, 2005).

Library of Congress Control Number: 2009930166
ISBN 978-0-88748-521-3 Pbk.
Printed and bound in the United States of America

10 9 8 7 6 5 4 3 2 1

Contents

from *Durations*, 1984

from *Groceries*, 1976

I. Learning the Business

from *Disguises*, 1974

from *Sleeping Woman*, 2005

I.

II.

III.

IV.

Foreword

Few lovers of poetry—practitioner or promoter (Herb was both)—have this much heart. Herbert Scott's poems are full of appreciation for beauty in a world that, at times, feels barely survivable. Herb knew plenty about the margins—the hardscrabble goings-on of the working class—from his life in Oklahoma, and then, later on, in Fresno. *Suffering is just part of the deal, so we'd better get used to it*, his poems say. Herb found human dignity everywhere. Living life as if every second counted—circumstances be damned—was his big subject, and so it makes sense that his work is populated with Gravediggers and Grocers (two occupations Herb was familiar with, as the poems attest). *The Other Life* is a book of prayers, stories, and meditations, and yet nothing in this volume comes across as precious, written as it is (and I mean, this is how the poetry *feels*) so brazenly out of experience.

Pick up *Groceries*, Herb's tough-edged version of *The Spoon River Anthology*. It's *One Flew Over the Cuckoo's Nest* with stocked shelves and a meat department. It's a captivating book of persona poems from the perspective of "Boss" and "Butcher" and less prestigious department heads such as "Canned Goods"—and it's a gritty, sometimes harrowing, often funny performance.

Speaking of humor in poetry, I love this poem from Herb's *Sleeping Woman*:

That Summer

That summer nothing would do
but we sink the boat
in the heart of the lake
and swim in the cool night
for the yellow fire on the beach.

Through the dark water.

We all made it but Ronald,
whom we never found,
who was never Ronald

again; each fish I catch
since, I ask *Ron, is that you?*

That "Through the dark water" gleams in this small piece of noir, deadly serious, and then the whole business is put into proper perspective in the last five lines: *Live, die, will you get real?* And all of it is couched in that inimitable voice, a bit of tenderness tucked into every corner.

Those who worked with him at New Issues Poetry & Prose, authors and volunteers and support staff alike, know how devoted Herb was to the art of the poem, how tireless he was, and how skilled he was as an editor. Herb had an uncanny ability to clarify the essence of a book of poems, to identify a poet's intent and shape it into something, somehow, more truthful-seeming—by cutting all the bullshit, or transposing a few key words or phrases, or arranging the poems in such a way that they better enacted a formal and thematic arc. Out of the confluence where author and editor meet, Herb was able to pull the best out of a manuscript of poems without muddying the waters of authorship, without staining it with his own poetic quirks or personality, as wonderful as both of those things were. And Herb loved it—the transformative process of sculpting and fine-tuning a poet's work into a finished book— as much as (and for a while, instead of) the process of writing his own poems.

There is no denying that Herb's work suffered for the sake of others. I don't believe the quality of the work was diminished, but Herb put his own poetry on the back burner for the better part of fifteen years. He wrote and published little during this time (an exception being 2001's *In the Palm of Space*, published by Sutton Hoo Press) because he was pouring his heart into his work at New Issues. His last book, *Durations*, had come out in 1984. More than twenty years would pass before he published his fourth, and final, collection, *Sleeping Woman*.

But if the work suffered in terms of quantity, Herb's last poems are hard with a deft authority, a simplicity that belies their emotional depths, a faith in the purposefulness of poetry, its ability to make something transcendent out of the given life, out of experience. The poems are intense and yet quietly precise; addresses of witness so seamlessly composed they feel effortless; perfectly constructed machines of words. And everywhere in Herb's poetry a deep awareness of death keeps sparking an overwhelming and answering *solace of possible love*, to use a phrase from the title poem of this volume.

These poems cut to the heart of the matter, and they do so with elegance and just the right turn of phrase—historical and wise, erotic and pastoral (I would argue that Herb was one hell of a nature poet); poems lit from within, songs and—I want to say again—prayers. Herbert Scott had so much faith in human beings, and he knew how to capture that in poem after poem.

Carnegie Mellon University Press planned to publish a selection of Herbert Scott's poetry several years back, and then that project became *Sleeping Woman*. (Probably this was for the best: *Sleeping Woman*, to my mind, is one of the best single-book collections to be published this decade.)

As to the arrangement of the book you're holding, in most cases I stuck to versions Herb was considering for that original selected poems. At the time, he and I had argued over what should be included. Herb was hard on himself. I was working to convince him to add more poems, and he was slowly—sometimes—reinstating poems he'd decided to remove. I have tried my best to include in this collection what I think, in the end, Herb would have wanted to include. I've relied, too, on advice from Shirley Clay Scott, Herb's wife, whose passion for Herb's poetry made this book possible.

I also made a few cuts in honor of the master pruner himself, my teacher, and I restored sections of "Dinosaurs" and "The Gravedigger's Apprentice." Before the project of a selected poems faded, Herb had seemed excited by the prospect of leaving some of the longer poems as written.

At least that is what I believe.

I'm not sure much of this matters, though. Herbert Scott wrote very few inconsequential poems.

David Dodd Lee
September 2009

from *Durations*, 1984

Achilles' Heel

The foot slides open, disjointed
toes askew, arteries spurting
legions of Greeks, Romans, the tribes
of Israel, Alexander, Hannibal,
and the long river we call *Helen.*
And the river rich with bodies, little flags
of hands protruding, the baby Moses, silt
that builds deltas at the mouth of darkness.

And the foot marking the throat of the slave
for the axe, for the hand to lift
the unencumbered head,
for the fingers never to be free again
of that wrath of hair.
The four-clawed foot
digging its terrible furrows. . . .

Or the slender, high bridge,
lacy, intricate arch, the lover's mouth
laid against the instep,
that curve of air, delicate slippage
along the long slip of thigh . . .
until all collapse
as the heel comes down,
shatters, as cities splinter,
as the foot turns, disembodied,
almost its own master.

The Woman Who Loves Old Men

She loves the brown moles
widening to pools of oil
on their faces, their eyes
turning to milk, the tiny
forests of their ears;

and the shoulders,
wearing thin as skulls,
the slow glaciers of flesh
sliding from bone;

and oh the white bellies,
the pure salt of their bellies,
she could bury her face forever
in such perfect snow.

Yes, she marries them,
and they roost in her arms
like tired birds as she listens
for the last drawn croak
before that certain stillness.

And they, thankful, never know
it is their deaths she loves,
their bodies she lays out
like polished wood, as she dreams
of the one who will marry her twice.

Fathers of Desire

We are fathers of the child
at its mother's breast,
the child who sleeps
in our doubled arms,
heavy and sweet.
This is a love we bless.

We are fathers of the child
on fire, who bears
no lips, no nose, no hair,
whose eyes will never close;
and fathers of desire.
No. We cannot forgive ourselves.

We are fathers of the child
who turns to stone, no heart
to moan into our ears
laid like flowers
against its chest. No one
loves us more than this.

The Dead

It is the dead who are always with us,
handsome and winning, on their best behavior.

We carry them in our chests
like an extra heart.

Companions who never falter,
who live in us their second lives.

And how can we deny them?
We who held them in our laps too long,

their languorous arms about our necks,
the breath of their sweet skin swarming.

How can we say:
This is the last kiss goodnight?

We who do not yet know
forgiveness was never possible.

Travelers

Who speaks in these cartoons
where the precipice
is simply a line
drawn off the page?

The flesh
is no harbor for joy.
It falls from us
like loose change.

Father, where
is your stern look?
Mother, your breasts
have flown away.

There is a distance
we cannot travel
between our hands
and the faces

of those we love.
Turn back, before
it is too late,
the girl screams

but the travelers
do not hear,
for the wind is blowing
her words into sky

as the camera swings
for a view
of the precipice
we anticipate.

The Past

We dreamt we nailed its coffin shut.
Awake, we know it waits for us
in the rooms of our deepest seclusions.

And we have learned nothing!
Not how to keep ourselves alive,
no hocus pocus . . .

When it slips into our beds, a former
lover, we feel how unfamiliar its skin is.
Yet we make love as if it were alive.

Again we know how all things fasten.
We have so much to say.
It will not listen.

The Future

Ignorance, our bloody
scribbled child, casts off
swaddling clothes,
struts naked in boiling skin.

On the Missouri

i.

Cottonwoods climbing the shore,
plumes of green smoke,
the little corks of fish popping . . .
There is no loneliness like this.
You forget where you came from,
The magic glitter of cities,
the lovely sweat of your loved ones,
the life you had courted and married.
In the steady pulse of the river
you learn patience,
like an old dog
who has learned to stand soberly
above his empty dish
somehow understanding
the unswerving disposition of time.

ii.

In the small towns along the river
we remember these things:
The story the river writes
on the walls of our houses.
How we lived on the roof for three days
and tied the dog to the chimney to save her.
The story of fish.
Where they come to shake your hand.
The quiet gullies of water
where you visit your deaf grandfather,
where you drift to sleep
until he stumbles over your feet
on the way to the kitchen.
Where to knock on water.
And how the mackerel sky, sometimes,
near sunset, is another river.

iii.

If you should leap suddenly into the river
and swim for shore
no one would know
where to forward your laundry
or the names of those who believe you loved them.
Only the far shore,
the bluffs like distant relatives,
the trees that will not stop growing,
will answer your call each morning
when you shout *good morning*!
And an old woman,
hunched beneath a cottonwood,
her heavy breasts riding her knees
like two fat babies,
will love you,
even before your teeth fall out,
even before you slip
into the muddy shallows
your tail slapping the water as you swivel.

Dinosaurs

Robert Plot, First Keeper
The Ashmolean Museum, 1677

Stones

I *have one*
dug out of a quarry
in the Parrish of Cornwell
and given me by the ingenious
Sir Thomas Pennyston,
that has exactly the Figure
of the lowermost part
of the Thigh-Bone *of a* Man
or at least of some other Animal.

It seems to have been broken off,
shewing the marrow within
of a shining Spar-like *Substance*
in the hollow *of the Bone.*
In Compass *near the* capita Femoris
just two Foot,
and at the top above the Sinus
about 15 inches; in weight,
though representing so short a part
of the Thigh-Bone, *almost 20 pounds.*

This Stone of ours
must have been a real Bone,
now Petrified.
It must have belonged
to some greater animal
than either an Ox *or* Horse;
and if so in probability

it must have been the Bone
of some Elephant, *brought hither*
during the Government of the Romans
in Britain.

      *

                    On the Weber River in Utah
                    July, 1977

On these shores
dinosaurs lay down to die
70 million years ago.

Their bones are stone
driven into stone.
It is dusk.

I sit on the ground
at the water's edge
writing these words.

Two boys in waders
fish beneath the low, curved bridge
downstream. Yesterday

they caught twelve bass,
threw them back,
the largest three pounds.

Today their luck is better.
What are you doing, they ask.

Broadleafed grass
grows in random clumps
among the stones.

The water is a voice

that cleans my bones.

                    *

> *"You have found the remains*
> *of an animal new to science."*
> *— Gideon Mantell*

A young woman walks
along a country road
in the Cuckfield district

of Sussex, while her husband
calls on a patient
dying of childbed fever

on an early spring
afternoon in 1822.
The woman pauses

at a pile of roadmetal,
bends down,
closes her hand

around a tooth
thick as a wrist bone
embedded in Tilgate stone.

I think of this
as an act of love,
Eva Mantell

affixing her small hand
to the tooth
of a dinosaur

lifting it from the earth

a gift for her husband
walking to meet her

from the bed of another woman
dying in the afternoon
sunshine of Sussex.

                *

This afternoon,
after driving all day

across the dry wash
of Colorado and Utah

I came upon this river
among the low hills,

narrow and swift,
harrowed by stones.

I shed my clothes and waded in,
lowering my body

into the channel.
The cold, fast water

seemed to startle me alive
again, taking my body down

the river, glancing
against rocks. I threw

my head back, laughing,
beating my arms

against the water,

laughing at my own

strange body,
featherless,

scaleless,
ground-blessed creature.

                   *

I came upon a woman
kneeling on the bank

washing her clothes,
her breasts rocking.

She leaned on her haunches,
looked at me and laughed,

now lifting her long
red hair like water

in her hands,
catching it behind her ears.

I laughed again, at her beauty,
at myself, and was not shy.

                   *

Later, lying back
on the grassy bank,

I watched the woman
lift her skirt

between her legs

tuck it at her waist

until it billowed
around her thighs

like bloomers. She waded
into the water

shaking her hair
loose, a red shower

across the belly
of the late afternoon sun

the sky stark blue
above green and brown hills.

And the stones kept
their perfect peace.

*

Three hundred years ago
John Lightfoot, Vice Chancellor
of Cambridge, announced

the date of Creation:
September 17, 3928 B.C.,
nine o'clock in the morning.

Archbishop Ussher of Ireland
preferred
October 23, 4004 B.C.

Now we need the earth to be
four billion years old, at least.

What can we know

in our insatiable ignorance?

          *

Here were dense swamps,
water lilies, horsetail rushes,
cypress, eucalyptus, fern.

On high ground, grape, laurel,
oak and sequoia, ebony,
bayberry, honeysuckle, ash.

Some lived in the marsh, thunder
lizards, fifty tons of flesh and bone,
heart the size of a woman,
bodies too heavy for dry land.

These were plant eaters,
duck-billed, bone-headed, beaked,
some with two thousand teeth,

tearing plants from the moist earth,
swallowing whole bushes,
young trees, rocks still clinging
to clods of soil around roots,

swallowing the rocks,
as much as a bushel of rocks
riding in the hold of the huge belly
grinding the plants to mulch.

Others lived on dry land,
lizard-hipped, meat eaters,
standing on two legs, swift,

powerful, some with skulls

six feet long
jaws strong enough to tear
whole limbs from live victims.

And all would grow back,
tree, vine, bush,
tendon, bone, flesh,

for 150 million years
all would grow back.

＊

In 1802, Pliny Moody
found tracks in red sandstone

believed to be those of a large bird:
Noah's raven.

And few would believe
the real miracle of bones
hauled from the earth.

Sports of nature.
Fabrications of the stars.

Working models:
practice for the Creation.

False, fearful bones,
hoax of an angry God
to frighten us into belief.

Yet a sheep herder in Wyoming
built a small cabin
entirely of dinosaur bones,

and others, farmers,

miners, railroaders,
finding these bones,

took them into their homes
as ornaments, door stops,
playthings for their children,
and were unafraid.

*

Each summer I travel west
along these highways

from Michigan to California
to see my children.

In Fresno, the buildings turn
their weathered skins to the sun.

Del Webb's new townhouse
already closed down.

I remember a worker tumbling
to his death, thirteen years ago,

the year I moved east
to a different life.

Madame Temple
still reads cards on the corner

of McKinley and Wishon.
I remember too well

her legend:
There is no pity

for those who need help

and do not seek it.

*

Gideon Mantell, I see you
digging your way for years
through secret quarries,

giving up the living
for the dead

bringing the dead
bones back, your patient hands
peeling the limestone

flesh away, until those bones
seemed to breathe
beneath the ancient, sweat-stained dust.

Each night you kept your vigil
until the sudden light
of dawn startled you.

Or perhaps you heard
Eva
turn in her sleep

and you'd lay down
beside her, for a moment,
surprised at her warm skin.

*

Last summer, leaving
the dry heat of the valley,

my youngest daughter and I

drove to the coast, Pismo Beach,

the wind cold off the ocean.
We walked along the edge

of the surf that washes in,
covering our feet and ankles,

looking for shiny rocks and shells.
I looked down at the sand

patterns on my daughter's back
as she bent to pick up a shell.

A good one.
She put it in my pocket,

heavy with the day's collection.
I laid my hand outside the pocket,

feeling the weight of it,
the sun going down,

my daughter beside me, the sand
giving beneath our feet.

*

Waterhouse Hawkins
fathered the first
dinosaurs, in 1853,

great horned monsters
resurrected from the deep
grasses of England.

Half a century later

Othniel Marsh would say

there is nothing like unto them
in the heavens, or in the earth,
or in the waters under the earth . . .

But they were true
children
of this world

the mortal imagination
giving birth
to those transfigured beasts.

> *

The boys wade
into the current.

Their arms snake out,
draw back, their voices

now and then

an indistinct music
above the water.

They must have been beautiful,
long, sinewy necks

muscle and bone
stirring beneath skin

the skin shining
like a morning dream.

> *

Along the highway
from Colorado

into Utah, cement
and stucco monsters

rise from their deaths
in front of curio stands

pink, purple, polka-dotted
skins, feeble grins

no terror, no beauty,
no belief.

And we have watched
across the earth

these great beasts rise
from celluloid seas

or in our homes
become

fists of light,
these poor excursions

our desire to know,
their loss, our loss

our names written in stone.
If we are afraid

it is for the drowse
of our lives

in which these dreams

may die.

*

At suppertime,
across a small meadow,

the red-haired woman bends
above her camp stove

bushes and branches
of trees about her

laden with bright clothes.
She looks up, smiles.

A man claims her,
circles her with his arms.

I turn away. I am lonely,
my wife asleep

in her warm body
two thousand miles away.

Later that night
she will come to my tent,

lie beside me, take
my hands to her body.

I smile at my foolishness
and sit down to supper.

*

You are still with me
after twenty years,
old woman, chanting

your story to Cunegonde
and Candide, on the way
to the new world.

You were taken
by a pirate captain
at fifteen,

your lover dead
in Massa-Carrara
of poisoned chocolates,

your mother, alive,
hacked to pieces
before your eyes.

You survived the plague
in Algiers, were sold into slavery,
raped a thousand times.

The starving Janizaries
who held you captive
during the siege of Azov

carved up
one of your buttocks
for food.

Growing old
in misery and shame,
only half a backside,

you say, *a hundred times*

I wanted to kill myself
but I still love life.

*

New Year's Eve, 1899
at the Crystal Palace

twenty-one scientists
gathered to celebrate

a new age of learning
within the belly

of a dinosaur:
Mantell's *Iguanodon*

the creation
of Waterhouse Hawkins

out of 600 bricks
650 half-round drain tiles

900 plain tiles
30 casks of cement

90 casks of broken stone
100 feet of iron hooping.

*

Why do we so love the body?

We carry the body within the body,
its small heart beating.

And then it comes.

And then it runs away.

Each year the gift
diminished

the darkness within
seeping through the skin.

Even after death we try to save the body.
The body in our arms.

Its well of breath gone dry.
The body in its disgrace.

                *

This morning at the diggings
near Vernal

where 300 tons of bones
have been taken from the earth

I studied the remains
of fourteen dinosaurs

chiseled into relief
on the tilted face

of the quarry.
A woman in a blue dress

lifted her young daughter
to stroke a pelvic bone.

30 tons, brain
the size of a kitten's.

77 inches from sole to scalp

I could curl up

inside that bone, become
its stone child.

*

How we desire the earth
to open and yield
those great bodies

full-fleshed and lovely
in the glint of the sun

for them to come back
to what they knew

not to be held captive
in preserve or sanctuary

but to live beside us
and we beside them
living in wonder.

Only the possum knows.
Ancient and slow

like a favorite grandfather
who no longer speaks

he waddles along
crossing the road
into the weeds.

*

In America,
Waterhouse Hawkins

raises his studio
in Central Park

to house the birth
of dinosaurs.

He will set them free
in that wild habitat,

a gift to the people
of New York City.

Somewhere beneath
that unredeemed wilderness

those half-formed monsters
keep.

                *

And I had forgotten
the blackbirds,
white-winged,

as large as grackles,
the most beautiful
I have seen.

All evening
I watched them along
the river, going

about their lives.

They are not scavengers.
They are not afraid.

They land beside me
as if there were a pact
between us. Perhaps

they like to watch me.
Perhaps I am beautiful
to them as they are to me.

Or at least amusing.
When the blackbirds take flight
the white markings

of their wings
flare and disappear
like hands among clothing.

   *

How can the body survive?
At night the hills receive
a different life,

texture changed to shadow.
Huge, stable bodies,
and what remains is form.

   *

Nine teeth, a lower jaw,
bits of the upper,

28 vertebrae, the bones
of fore and hind limbs

dug from a marl pit, in 1858,

near Haddonfield, New Jersey

the first partial skeleton
unearthed in America.

Waterhouse Hawkins
married the bones

to plaster, to each other,
the head his own

invention. Waterhouse,
they broke these bones

down, in 1940,
laid them out

in a small glass case
in Philadelphia.

        *

A car climbs the road
through the trees.

All I can see
are its headlight beams
tugging at the sky.

The boys pack up their gear,
wave goodbye,

walk from the river
to the road

the light coming down

from the sky

leveling, catching them
for a moment in its eye.

Now they are gone
with their luck

and their fish
and their slick wet boots.

        *

The dinosaurs died
in a geological instant.

*A huge comet
loomed past the sun*

*sweeping the earth
with its tail.*

*Stinging insects.
A great ice age.*

*The earth rose up
and the marshes drained.*

*Nothing to eat.
Nothing to eat.*

*Primitive mammals
sucked their eggs dry.*

They lay down like bathers
after a long swim.

        *

And you, Gideon Mantell,
died alone in a house full
of bones, in London.

Eva had left you.
Not enough room
in the house of bone.

The earth laced with bones.
Clean, cold bones, coming apart.

Here we are, singing
this mad opera

the story the usual
melodrama

the saving grace
of earthly music.

                    *

Who will name us?
How will we be known?

Will some life form
lift us from the earth
love our puny bones

these sticks
that won't bring fire,
carve them

into implements, ornaments,

unfold these arms
crossed against our chests

as if we could
hold in
death?

                    *

I am alone
with the river.

The moon,
a cup of light.

The working water
will not rest.

Something downstream
catches my eye,

comes slowly
towards me,

rising and falling
in the half-light.

Something alive
is all I know,

climbing the river.

                    *

Now I see

the muskrat

tail flashing
above the water,

disappearing, something
held in its mouth,

her young in her mouth.
She doesn't notice me

as she climbs
belly over stone

intent against the pull
of the river, the water

sucking her fur.
Primitive, essential

motion, learned
through centuries

of survival,
ordinary and beautiful

blood and bone
and wet fur.

*

She passes within
my arm's reach

her body gleaming,
leaping, dipping.

I could touch her,

the wet, sleek body,

but I would not.
For a space I have become

invisible
to other creatures.

*

There is a beauty
that rises from bodies

indescribable!
mingling with air and darkness.

We are its familiar gestures,
its words already spoken.

*

The water seems spun
to a delicate fiber
pulled over a loom

words only a memory
already distant

water spinning its way
past the muskrat

lugging her young
up the river.

She disappears, the night
too dark to see

these words

pushed across the page.

*

I stand up
beside the water
and think of my wife

remembering
that summer morning
we walked

on the dark beach
at Pine Point, Maine,
before dawn,

wanting to see
the sun rise
above the Atlantic,

the sand cold ashes
beneath our bare feet.

We strolled,
arm in arm,
near the water,

looking out
to Prout's Neck

where Homer stood
in the flung surf

painting the pure fury

of our beginning.

*

I leave the river
and walk back to camp.

I can hear voices
again, laughter,

fire breaking wood
into coal and ash.

I crawl into my tent,
settle down among covers.

This small space is enough.

Kalamazoo, Michigan
May 1978

The God That Keeps Us Alive

i.
Love, in whose honor
we grow towards the sky

in whose service
we diminish death

Love, on whose journey
we map ourselves,
the bodies of our mates

husband the grassy fields
where we feed
the pools where we swim

the shoals of bone
where we draw shelter

Love, we bend
to kiss you

becoming gods ourselves,
though not gods, and dying.

ii.
We mark our ascent
in kitchen doorways

in our children,
their shoes empty
as our lives would be.

Winter comes.

Trees die in this season

fall in the deep snows
unseen, unheard.

Beneath our feet
the earth shudders.

iii.
Love, brief father
who leaves us
orphans in dry rooms

winter heat
cracking our bones . . .

We are warriors
of loss

falling
in the streets
of foreign cities.

You lick our wounds,
the salt healing,
the blood remembering.

iv.
Love, you are
nearly great enough.

The myth you father
is worth the living.

Early Love

for Emma

Your skin was blue-
puddle snow, I mean
so fine I could trace
your flow from every
tributary. Your breasts,
yes, they were truthful,
freckled and new
beneath your shirt
that summer afternoon
we climbed the ladder
to the barn's dark loft.
We lay down
in the sweet straw
your body
granting the darkness
such mercy
until your brother,
shouting,
brought us down
to fish for crawdads
below the garden.
Your brother,
and your dead sister,
forever between us.
To be with you
I had to pretend
your brother
was my close friend.
On summer nights
we three slept on the lawn
beneath the open sky,

your brother
the dark body
in the center,
we, like wings,
never touching,
unless
I would fling
one arm
in a long arc
across the sky,
perhaps I saw a meteor,
my descending hand
brushing your shoulder,
and you would laugh
and touch my hair
in tender retaliation.
I suppose
you were lonely,
put up with us,
with me
who tugged at you,
innocent and severe,
wanting your skin
to grow around me.
Then your older sister
married and died
within the year.
After the funeral
her husband came for you,
claimed you
from your father
as if you were payment
for that death.
You were sixteen
the day you were taken
by a man in a straw hat

straight-backed
your arms full
of folded clothes
on the front seat
of his car.
I could see everything
from the south pasture
where I lay
tear-shaken, spying
on your leaving,
your solemn descent
from view. I never again
slept with your brother.

Oklahoma Sunset

In the meadow, quail
rattle the beaded grass.

An old man and old woman
nod each other daft.

We listen
to the day's even breathing.

Hives of lilac buzz
in the languorous sunset

the sky's correct
spelling of *evening*.

Woman with Pitcher

How carefully
her hands
describe
the stoneware
pitcher
how it empties
and fills
the stir
of water
inside
a swirl
of shadow
and light
her hands
taking
and giving
the water
forming
its body
as the wheel
turns
as the wet
clay climbs
the pantomime
of her hands.

The Ceremony of the Ducks

On the closing of the Peabody Hotel
Memphis, 1978

i.
And there was music
in their squawk
and clatter

her laughter
blowing

a white feather
from her lips

as he unbuttoned
the winged collar
of his shirt

his boots sprawled
on the floor
like drunken friends.

ii.
They were
a gift for her

their flutter and walk
each morning
rousing her from dreams.

And he would waken
to her body
feathered in light

her nipples
two notes
on a white page

and to joy
in his own
surprised laughter

as she mimicked
their strut
across the room

her face
over her shoulder

favoring him
with its tiny explosions.

iii.
High above the city
in this Eden
he must leave

each morning
to pay the rent
that he may keep her

she would, barefoot,
walk them to the door,
her sweet babies,

and tie his tie
and kiss his lips.

And could she help
but laugh, watching
that earnest procession

to the elevator
his foolish smile
that took her breath.

iv.
Curled in bed
beneath the morning
drift of light

she closed her eyes
on his way down

and knew his bending
his stroking

those waxy,
skittering backs

like the turn
of her own thighs

the tattoo
of orange beaks
against his legs.

v.
And she remembered
his lifting
the wicker picnic hamper

from the crook
of a street boy's arm
that summer morning

sending
two silver worlds
spinning in sunlight.

Later, spilling
those lively dancers

into her lap
like popped corn!

vi.
She knew
how they would tack
across the lobby,

a tiny flotilla,
swim all day
in the foyer fountain

her lover nearby
in his starched collar

smoothing his moustache
above the counter.

vii.
At dusk
they would return,
her clamorous family,

to chase her laughter
about the room

a snow of feathers
scattering like sneezes

catching
the falling light.

viii.
How well
he loved her

to bring her
such sleek creatures

for her arms
for her breasts

for her white waddle!

The Man Who Would Be a Mother

The stirrings in his chest
are maternal, mild. He imagines
giving suck, the gentle ooze,
the child's lips still forming
around his nipple. He wipes away
the last drop with his thumb,
lifts it to his tongue. Milk.
The first taste in his mouth again.

He would say to his children:
You were once in my belly. This
is how you fed before you were born.
This is where I held you,
child on a rope of blood.
This is my mark on your belly.
When you came into your life,
they held you up for me to see,
as if I were dangling from you, your child.

If I am not your mother,
and you do not rise from my body,
it is not because I would not have it.
Take my hands, as if they were
your face, and when I am dead,
and this flesh unlocks the bones,
imagine birth from my body,
a garden of children blooming.

As She Enters Her Seventieth Year
She Dreams of Milk

i.
An early mist
rises

from the mute
curdled brain
of earth

Milk wakens
and speaks
its name

common
as semen

ii.
She remembers
her mother

a white flame
in the dark house

bringing anise
in hot milk

evening prayers
in flannel gowns

her mother bending
above the bed

like a pitcher
pouring

porcelain cups
steaming

their licorice
breath

iii.
And was it
her lover

who knelt
beside her

in the unlit
room

taking
her breast

to his large
face

when she, waking,
felt

the pulse
of milk

within
her chest

iv.
Her husbands
loved

her lush
full breasts

their oyster
mouths

the nipples'
push

against
her blouse

v.
She loved
the mothy sleep
of children

on the slopes
of their fathers

the fish flesh
of wet muzzles

her babies
in their cribs

dream-sucking
the mammal

memory
of milk

vi.
She knows
the tatting

of the cat's
tongue

at the rim
of milk

the blue light
that brims

beneath
the white skin

how milk is grass
and blood

the teeth
of wolves

on clear nights
how the heavens flood

vii.
She knows
how milk comes
and goes

body
the wheel

where babies
turn

how the flesh
will wean

and soon
decay

how nothing
remains

but bone
the stone

of milk
its hard home

viii.
Old woman
she names
herself

heavy
breasts

swelling
at her waist

like heads
of cheese

one more mouth
to feed

ix.
She bows
her head

and milk
peers up
at her

with its calm
face

The Other Life

In this poem
a man walks along the street
through a neighborhood of familiar nods,
extrapolations of trees. In this neighborhood
there are no sidewalks as stern reminders,
no salesmen lugging their heavy lives
door to door. Only windowsills of sanguine
demeanor, the green addendum of lawn.

The man pauses at the door
of a house he will enter. On the couch
a coat he might have worn, on the rug some slippers.
From the arrangement of light he knows
this room has a memory of dear occasions.
In the kitchen someone has buttered
toast on a porcelain saucer, set
a beaded pitcher of milk on the table.

Those who were once here will be close by,
children with little tusks of milk pointing,
a woman sipping butter from the tips of her fingers.
And when he finds them, those expectant faces,
those hands folded in laps
like bows on Christmas boxes,
he will say, yes, you have done well,
this is the way it was meant to be.

And they will be happy, too,
long years of not knowing behind them,
knowing now that neither time nor separation
is the final measure of joy.
That night, in the various rooms of this house,
they will kiss each others' lips,

turn back the thick, dark covers,
lie down in a solace of possible love.

from *Groceries*, 1976

The Shoplifter's Handbook

Directions

Keep your head on straight, let your eyes
be rovers. Indecision breeds suspicion.
If you know where you are going, get there.

Meat puts muscle on your frame.
Endow yourself if God didn't.
A cod piece for your crotch,
a brace of filets for your chest.

Slip oysters in your pockets but not sardines.
A broken arm slings a chicken.
Fold the *News* around a steak.

Remember, good things come in small packages.
Cigarettes go up in smoke,
eye shadows disappear in purses,
pills and purges leave no trace.

Precautions

Take only what you can conceal.
It's a free country. You may return
an empty bottle, fill up again,
become a regular customer.

Carry no identification, labels, fingerprints,
pictures of loved ones, birthmarks.
Forget your name. Remember your sex.
If you become confused,
touch yourself gently between the legs.

If you get caught,
choose a new name to plead your case:
Amanda, worthy to be loved, Manfred,
peace among men. Later you may need
Delores of sorrows, Hector holding fast.

Guilt

The time will come
you will grow a hand on your shoulder,
walk with a limp, surprise yourself
in the mirror. Disguise. Dye hair.
Fake a moth of a moustache feeding
beneath your nose. You think it's real
until it flies away.

You have a pocketful of moths, of holes,
your clothes are full of openings.
You fear that everything will show,
will come alive, chickens wing
from your arms, your body leak,
soft goods rise like kites
to string you from the ceiling.

Confession wags your tongue. Clip its tail.
You want purity and nakedness.
Give to charity what you can't use or sell.
Store up credit and good will. Begin again.

Warning

Trust no one. You have no friends.
Your appetite empties pockets, the cost
of living balloons from your breath.
Can you walk a straight line?

No one will pass this test.

Accessories

Your children grow hands like empty plates.
Hold them upside down, they sprout
a possum pouch. Lick their snouts
until they learn to smell each other out.

Let their teachers try to pry them open.
They remain closed as apples.
Take a bite. Their eyes and mouths are white.
Chew into the seeds, you'll spit them out.

Leave them in their skins, you nurtured them.
There's nothing you can do
to change the way their fingers grow.

Alibis

I am your long lost son, your daughter.
Don't you remember me, Father?
My sister's sick mother's giving birth.
A catastrophe fell off the shelf into my shirt.
It's the first time I forgot to pay.
They made me do it, my starving children,
my lame dog, my drunken father
who beats me with a hose.
I want to see a priest, my dead mother,
the President. Please forgive me. Forgive me.

I. Learning the Business

Opening Up

Boss turns on one light
above the safe,
a closed fist. He kneels
to the ceremony
of money, the morning sun
edging across the street,
the first customer
knocking at the door.
Boss plants the tills,
seed money, the new crop,
clips his black bow tie
like tiny wings across
his throat, whistling
between his teeth.

Butcher slings a hindquarter
on the block,
hones his long knife.
He knows where the bones
knuckle. The red angels
on his apron turn black.
Drums of bone and fat
fill for the rendering
plant truck. Everything
reduced to profit.
The wrapper spins a new skin
around steaks and chops. Butcher
catches her up against
the meat block, pinches
her ass. A slow dance
of carcasses, lamb, beef,
hog on heavy hooks.

The checker leans

into her stall,
hands on hips,
studies a list of specials,
as the lights come on
in glassware, pet foods,
paper, household, and dairy.
Boss unlocks the automatic
door. The first customer
pulls a cart from the rack,
pushes down produce,
stands quietly for a moment,
three bright hard lemons
in one hand.

The Childhood of a Grocer

On Saturdays my old man
give me and my brothers
each a dime
and them as wanted
hiked ten mile
to the country store
bought loaves
of fresh baked bread
quart jars of mustard
loafed the afternoon
in sycamore shade
in the haze of blue hills
rolling bread into balls
to savor the pucker
of mustard on our tongues.

Boss

I am one of the old line.
No one give me nothing.
I earned what I earned
and stole what I stole.
I know this business

like a beetle knows shit.
You got to live in it.
You got to smell it
like the sweat under your arms.
I smell groceries everywhere I go.

I love groceries,
the women coming in
lonely as hell.
The rich, the ugly,
the beautiful, the sweet,

they all walk through
them doors.
You want a education
you come to the right place.
We all got to eat.

Thief

A big-boned woman
heavy breasted
slips a boneless steak
in each bra cup.
Butcher grabs her
drags her back
behind the cooler.
She goes nuts,
makes him
go in, screams
bloody murder
as he pulls her breasts
out too. He slaps her
on the face
to shut her up.
"You got to get tough,
these broads,
they'll steal the pants
right off your ass."
Boss feels up the steaks,
warm as toast.
"Medium rare," he says.

Butcher's Dream

I seen a cat once,
its head pasted
to the pavement
by the wheel of a car,
but its legs don't know it,
the whole body scrambling
to get up, to get loose.
I always wished I could work
with live meat, the red salt
crusting on my wrist.
I should of been a doctor.
I used to worry
what is the tenderest part
of the human carcass.
Then I seen some cannibal said,
the palm of the hand.
A delicacy you can't find
in other game. He'd kill
for the human hand.
How do you figure?
Not even a meal.
But it makes you wonder.
It makes you look
at your own hand
like a strange animal.

Boss on the Floor

No one knows how Boss
keeps out of jail.
Boss, cupping a buttock

as he explains the merits
of Maxwell House coffee.
Boss, brushing a nipple

reaching for Van Camps
pork and beans. Boss, excusing
himself down the narrow aisles.

Boss on his knees
stocking his hand up a leg
as he comments on the sunny weather.

Boss's Dream

She come in one morning,
sassy as spring. I said,
Mam, you sure got long legs.
She smiled. I said, I bet
they come together
like the intersection
of Cedar and Vine. She said,
I bet you know the way
to get there from here.
We drove west of town,
back into Beecher's woods,
walked a quarter mile
through brush, wild grape
and onions, piled leaves under
a cottonwood shedding fur,
her legs branched out.
It was good in there.
Later, she had to take
a leak, squatted down
in the leaves and pissed
in her shoes. All the way
back to the car, her shoes
squishing, laughing to beat hell.
The best it ever was.
I'd of give her the keys to the store,
but she never come back.

Good Fresh Country Eggs

Forty-acre farmers bring eggs to market
in milk pail, basket, cases
layered like cakes, gathered from nests
perched high above king snakes,
skunks, egg-sucking dogs and cats;
or stolen from weeds where would-be mother hens
stash them away to hatch a family.
"Laid this morning," the farmer says.

We read the eggs by candle light,
four moons in each hand shine
translucent, clear and fresh,
someone's breakfast. "Yolks that
stand up and holler *good morning*,"
the farmer says. In others

the foetus curls, an old drunk,
suspended in liquid, does a dead man's
float. We crack them, skulls in a bucket,
stillborn children. The news travels
through your nose. "Good fresh country
eggs," the farmer says. "None of your
city eggs with crap all over.
Country chickens know how to wipe their asses."

Merchandising

Butcher's knife
skins the bone
white as neon.

He doesn't throw
anything away.
No one knows

what goes in
hamburger.
Something old

he bleeds it in,
educated his customers
to use it up

before the gas
blows it up.
Butcher cuts

his chickens
on the saw.
Breasts grow attached

to the ribs,
the thigh to the back.
If he could stick

a piece of tail
to the leg
he would.

Red Meat

"The counter life of fresh meat is three days."

Two days under
fluorescent lights
meat turns gray
as the skin of rats

slate-colored steaks
laid out for viewing
like dead fathers

mourners passing
shaking heads, lamenting
the high cost of survival.

The third day
we turn the other cheek,
expose a new side

you only imagined
existed. "They look
so natural," you say.

We are artists.
The flesh glows
health for another day

haloed
by a wreath
of fresh greens.

Hams

A woman brings a ham back.
She found maggots
eating Easter dinner.

A display of twenty hams
against the wall,
fat dripping down.

Each one unwrapped finds
maggots burrowed in.
We pour Clorox on the tiles,

behind the baseboard.
Armies of maggots boil out.
Butcher wipes the hams

in vinegar, wraps them up
marked down by ten percent.
We sell them all.

Six-Month Review

You ain't naturally gifted
in the sales and service line.
Hell, you couldn't sell
beans to a fart hound.

You got to work on your strong points.
You can spell, but too bad
you can't write worth shit,
no one can read the signs you hang.

What can you do? Work the checkstands,
stack cans, trim vegetables, sort bottles.
I suspicion you got a head
on your shoulders. Who needs it.

Don't smart ass the customers.
Sack the cans on bottom the eggs on top.
Fill the empty shelves, don't stand
around your thumbs in your belt.

Keep your apron clean and your pockets honest.
You'll make it all right, you'll live to be forty.

II. The Grocer's Children

Bag Boy

Bag Boy whips
the sacks open
with one flick
of his wrist,
moving his body
like a matador,
a little dance
he does
free of charge.
He is the best
and knows it,
using both hands,
the cans leaping
into the bag
in perfect arcs,
an item for every space,
the bag packing
straight and solid,
frozen foods separate,
the bread on top.
Customers love Bag Boy.
He lets them crunch
their own potato chips.

Pet Foods

Pet Foods has a woman,
comes in every day,
wants to know the difference
between meat and meat by-products.
She leans her elbows on her cart,
one high-heeled foot hooked
on the axle. Pet Foods swears
he can hear her nylons
rubbing on her thighs
as she rocks her legs.
She wants to know
do milk bones really clean the teeth.
She's thinking about getting
another dog, she buys so much
dog food. Boss says he's going
to move Pet Foods to glassware,
pick up the sales of jellies and jam.

Checker

Checker is beautiful,
dark, shiny hair,
breasts gentle as mares'
noses, easy gaited.
She doesn't like it
when Pet Foods
grabs her breasts
in the back room.
She knees him in the groin.
"They think you're meat
and they're bone," she says.
But she doesn't mind Bag Boy
feeling her legs
behind the checkstand
when he reaches for the sacks.
She knows he's not serious,
just passing the time of day.

The Clerk's Dream

I'm going to save
my money and someday
buy a store in the neighborhood.
Me and my wife will run it,
I'll be my own boss.
And when I take money
out of the till
it will be my own money.
And I'll open when
I feel like it,
and close when I feel like it.
I'll wear a flannel shirt
and no tie, and when my kids
get home from school
they'll stock the shelves,
they'll be cute as shit
in their little aprons,
and wait on customers.
I figure I'll make
maybe twenty grand a year,
and I'll join the Junior Chamber
of Commerce, and maybe
the Lions. I'll let my wife off
one afternoon a week
to play cards with the Jaycee
Janes, and on Christmas
I'll pack a apple box
with bent cans and busted cereal,
and maybe even a turkey,
and take it to the church
to give to them less
fortunate.

Coffee

"We grind our own."

You have to drink
coffee, or no one
survives ten o'clock.
Your shriveled eyes
are plumped up by coffee.
You do not regret
the brown stain
of moss on your teeth,
your hot tongue,
an otter swimming
the polluted river
of your throat.

Can you dream
the Amazon, the jungles
of Brazil pushed back
by coffee,
the intolerable morning sun
rising before breakfast
like a fat American,
while the hard, stained
fingers of natives
rattle you awake
to a full cup
of black coffee?

Dairy

Dairy likes to tell
about the day
a lady found a rat
in a half gallon
of milk.
He lectures us
on the importance
of rotating
perishable merchandise,
always putting
the new product
behind existing stock,
so nothing spoils.
"Now you take
a milk rat," he says,
"let it get old
and blinky,
it can taste
purely terrible.
Wouldn't want it
on *your* table,
would you?"

Relief Locations Manager

Relief is everywhere
at once. He's on his way
up. When he works the front,
the register jumps
under his fingers,
groceries flashing past
like landscape,
his arms almost
screaming with motion.
If he comes to help you
in your section, you know
you're moving too slow.
You go home ashamed
of your thick, clumsy hands.
Relief's bucking for manager
in a new store. You hope
he'll make it.

Glassware

I do the job
the best I can.
You won't find
a jar out of place.
All the labels
faced forwards,
no dust on *my* shelves,
I use the feather
twice a week.
I want to make Relief
at least before I'm thirty.
I don't know why
people don't pick up
more pickles and dressings.
We had a rainy summer,
I guess.
If you get a chance
to teach me the books,
on my own time,
I sure would appreciate
that. I had two years
at the junior college.
I'd like to learn
all I can about the business
so if something opens up
at least I can get
a handle on it.

Produce's Mouse

One old mouse
he come every night
to climb the rack
and nibble corn.
Only the sweetest
freshest ears
would he eat. I try
to catch that mouse
seven days a week,
a year I try
but he just keep
coming up the rack
tasting the corn
like the table was set
for him. And no
poison would he touch
no trap would he spring
but like it was special
he eat the cheese
with his corn
and I never did catch
the son of a bitch.

Produce and Relief

Produce tends
the vegetables
like a mother

caring for
small children,
peeling the leaves

from lettuce
with the gentle touch
of comforting a hurt

and with thick fingers
caressing the veins
of a cabbage head.

Relief, like an ant,
works around Produce
as if a rock were in his way

flicking his knife
through the vegetables
with nervous intensity

never pausing
except to flip
a grape or cherry

into his mouth
his tongue curling
like a lizard's.

Yesterday, over a crate

of fresh turnips,
Produce coldcocked Relief.

Grazing

... wearing our appetites in our eyes ...

We learn to live
off the fat of the land,
apricots pink as thumbs,
the hearts of melons
the color of tongues,
filling our mouths
with the sweet flesh
of Crenshaws, Casabas,
the delicate meat
of apples, pears, freestone
peaches. We eat our way
across America, Santa Rosa
plums, Paw Paw concords,
Indian River oranges,
the names of our ancestors
floating in the air
like pollen, Tartarian,
Coachella, D'Anjou, Thompson.
We learn the hand is a thicket
for berries, a field of peanuts,
an arbor for grapes.
Seeds litter the floor
like spent bullets.
We have survived again.

In the deserts of California
the tossing fruit is gentled
by the hands of migrants,
their transient children,
strapped into line
on the belts of conveyors,

the sun nailed shut
beneath lids of crates
shipped across America.
There is no more open range,
no wild persimmon, plum,
black raspberry. Fields
are being paid not to bear
children, crops ploughed under,
chickens and hogs bulldozed
into open pits. But here
is the hallelujah tree
dropping its fruit across
our paths. Come. Fill
your apron like a cornucopia.
Take the sun between
your teeth. Let it shout
to your tongue, a comrade in joy.

The Pig Man

The pig man comes
once a day to haul
the garbage. Perched high
on his throne of swill

he is the king
bringing
his heavy princesses
to roll the cans.

Oh to have girls
so thick and strong
to lift lard drums of swill
like baskets of wash!

The fat bastard
should have had sons
to be the men
his daughters are.

Butcher's Wife

Butcher's wife
weighs 300 pounds
is crazy jealous.
Saturday nights
he gets drunk
and lays a whore.
Later, at home, his wife
pulls off his pants
and shines a flashlight
on his pecker,
sniffs it, grabs his balls
and won't let go
until he confesses,
slaps his face
to make him sober up
enough to fuck her.
Next morning
for breakfast
she fixes him
eggs and toast
and waffles
a big center slice
of fried ham.

Boss's Father

When my old man died
he fell over in the field
like a blasted stump.
They come to get him,
the sirens whining,
the high point
of his life. So dumb
he couldn't even say *ambulance*.
He told them doctors
the *avalanche* come
to carry him away.
They must of passed that story
a thousand times
around the hospital,
them nurses and them mop boys
laughing their asses off,
my old man pissing out his life
all the while. I'm telling you
there ain't no end
to the ignorance in this world.

Canned Goods

You get near forty
they give you cans,
the heaviest job
in the store.
They don't want you around
when you're slowing down.
They got the last one
on a heart attack.
Forty-three.
Those bastards know
what they're doing.
You either walk out
or they carry you out.
I put in for crackers and cookies.
You think I'll get it?
Not a chance.

Canned Goods' Dream

When I was a kid
we bunked in one room
piled two and three a bed
the beds lined up like desks
in the country school.
I slept with my sister
closest to me. That night
I could see her eyes
move like rabbits in moonlight,
then fix on mine, knowing
I was there. I knowed
she could smell the heat climbing
from my body. Her hands
beat on my sides as I come down.
She tried to take me
without crying, her small body
tough as hickory,
but the cry come, strange
and long, as I felt her give
and fell into her
for the first time in my life.
She lay humid and warm
like a summer night,
the sky deep in stars.
Who can say we knowed any better?

Sunday

Sunday morning
we go to work
before the Catholics
go to church.
We wash, we wax
the floors, trim vegetables
down, the brown leaves,
cracked stalks renewed
by water and the knife.
You could lie down
and die on the empty shelves
in the deep pit of Sunday
while somewhere women
wind their long hair,
the faces of their men
luminous in the cold
electronic light, the children
in their rooms practicing
what we already know,
all of us listening,
listening with bent heads
to the sermon of our lives.

The Grocer's Children

The grocer's children
eat day-old bread,
moldy cakes and cheese,
soft black bananas
on stale shredded wheat,
weeviled rice, their plates
heaped high with wilted
greens, bruised fruit,
surprise treats
from unlabeled cans,
tainted meat.
The grocer's children
never go hungry.

Closing Up

The sunset like a cut throat.
The night bleeds white,

flecks of milk in its mouth,
the tongue you sing to.

Your face in the window,
looking in

a tie slung over
your shoulder like a rope.

Going home, you fall into your wife
like a torrent of stars.

III. The Fear of Groceries

The Fear of Groceries

A man goes to a grocery store to buy
a can of peaches. Returning home
and opening the can for his supper
he discovers not peaches, but a heart.
He slumps to the floor of his kitchen
holding the heart in his lap like a fish.
The label, he checks again, reads *peaches*,
he is sure, or does it say *fishes*?
He looks at the fish in his lap,
his finger hooked in its mouth.
Very much like a heart, he says.
He bends his head to cry and sees
his children's faces reflected in the red eyes
of the heart, the glossy, salmon heart.
His children are spawning,
or drowning in an ocean, their faces
very like the halves of canned peaches.

Edna

She wheels her tire
through the streets of town
in her flower-print dress
and tennis shoes.

She doesn't speak,
but smiles at everyone.
No one knows
where she lives,

who pays her wages.
At noon she stops
by the store,
parks her tire at the curb,

a B. F. Goodrich,
puts her money down
a Double Cola,
Hostess Cupcake lunch.

She lifts the bottle like a horn.
The song she plays is short.
A workman's lunch
leaning on the plate glass

store front, driving off,
her one-wheeler
taking her down
familiar roads.

Schooling

Late afternoon the children
come in from school.
All day they have eaten
the sorrow of small rooms
the tragedy of textbooks
until their stomachs spin
like the skies over battlefields.

In the sweet aisles
their empty hands
pulse like hearts
their bodies open like gates
to fill with the flood of goods.
At suppertime they founder
in the laps of their fathers.

Hands

A man is putting on his hands.
They have grown soft as old potatoes.
He can't do a thing with them.
He found them in his neighbor's yard,
his neighbor's wife. They are old bones.
They are skin trying to make sense.
He gives them one more chance
not to make money, not to kill.
They empty his pockets. They finger him.
He is trying to remember if they are his hands.
If he puts them to his face
will they cup his eyes like pools?
Can he drink from them, will they feed him?
These hands shake in his lap,
buried in the fresh linen.
His wife took his left hand. His wife said,
I am your right hand. Which hands are his,
which body from the closet did they choose?

The Lost Aisles

There are aisles
we have not discovered
where a man and woman
are making love.
We hear her calling
his name, his name
is a song falling
beneath our feet.

All who enter
the lost aisles
must walk barefoot,
must carry
what they own,
must own their voices
lifting in praise.

In the lost aisles
when the lovers
have finished
the man lies still
within the woman, waiting
for her to rouse.
She does not push
him away, but holds him

in her arms
and legs, holds him
like a tree, the fruit
still falling around them.
They may eat
without leaving
each other's bodies.

The lovers may be lost
in any aisle
we cannot discover,
they may be waiting
for us to come, gather
the fruit in our arms,
gather them in our arms.

Cracked Eggs

"Any cracked eggs today?"
The old woman lifts her face
to me like a cratered moon.
I shake my head. Later,

in the back room,
I find her sucking
cracked eggs, a bucket
of them at her feet,

plucking the shells
from between her teeth
like the stems of strawberries,
a beard of yellow on her chin.

Surprised, she stutters an excuse,
broken speech twisting
like bones in her throat,

then hurries to the door,
old mother, wrapping
the shambles of her dignity
in the flapping wings of her coat.

Home Delivery

You have been here before.
She lets you in, whispers clues
in your ear, the missing
child, the dog that ate
the birthday, the bird
trapped in the refrigerator.
You reassure her, say
it doesn't matter.
But she is lonely,
and she bares her breasts,
and you take her nipples
between your teeth.
Now she remembers you,
the one who tattoos
flowers on her neck,
and she gives herself
one last time
for old times' sake.
When you leave, kicking
the mud from your boots,
you hear her calling
a name you don't remember.

Boss's Lament

This ain't no business for old men.
Look around. Show me the men
over fifty. You got to be young
and easy looking. You got to have
the glad hand and the sweet hello,
a smile as pretty as a mother's fart.

Someday I'll eat shit and not spit
it out. I'll want my job too much,
or end across the street washing dishes,
a bottle in my pants. The personality boys
will take my place. No more you don't
need to know nothing about groceries.

Armed Robbery

1. The Stock Clerk

The last time I filled
my pants I was thirteen,
my old man booted me
through the screen door
for touching my sister
I slept with in the same
room, the same bed.
What do they expect?
I hid my trousers under
a rock next to a blackjack
oak, let them rot away.
He never got near me again,
enough to kick my ass.

But I saw his face flash
like a grease fire
in the eyes of that bandit,
and I remembered.
The gun turned in my back
like a key, everything let loose
like a gravel slide
down Black's mountain.
I only got one pair of pants
fit to work in. My wife cried
when she saw them, unlaced
my shoes to pull them down.
They'll never come clean.

2. *The Checker*

When he touched me
with the cold blue barrel
of that gun, I thought
my skin would part.
I never knew such heaving
since my son turning,
pushing in my womb.
It felt like birth,
the hot pulse
stroking my thighs.
I felt taken, and given.
I gave what I could,
all he asked for.
I lay down wanting
whatever death he could offer,
wanting to be pinned
like an insect, a tattoo
on his chest. I will carry
his face chiseled in me
like a stone child, a jewel.
It's something maybe
never happens to you
once in your life,
if you survive it.
I know I could
have made him happy.

3. The Manager

I didn't want to see
his face. Show me
a picture of the gun,
it weighed a thousand pounds,
had a blue complexion,
didn't have to say a word.
I knew how to feed it.
Yes, I'm glad to be alive,
say hello to my wife
and my pet rabbit,
you stupid fuckers.
You want a hero
go over to the stadium
and pay your money
like everyone else.
You can shove these keys
if you think they mean more
than a way to pay the rent.
No sir, I couldn't say
"Yessir" fast enough.
I'm in this business to stay alive.

from *Disguises*, 1974

The Apprentice Gravedigger

"You'll always have a job."

1

There is a place for every body.
The Rich have frontage on the road;
the Masons sleep together in neat rows;
the Black lean back in weeds,
beyond the grass, where spotted
ground squirrels burrow in their holes.

2

Three feet of dirt,
two of clay,
the last, gray slate
that's hard to chip away.

We dig them clean and straight
as if our lives depended on it.

3

Two buddies
roared their bikes
beneath a cement mixer
and mixed their bodies.

No telling who
was where or what.
They dug out.
I dug them in.

4
The mourners come,
a fluttering of clothes,
in loose formations
through the stones

like birds that search
for scattered seed
on wintered fields.

5
Six months and three hard rains
the boxes go,
the earth caves in.

Wood rots as good
as man, I think.

The ground now knows
its tenant, not by
reputation.

We truck dirt in
and fill the graves again.

6
T.C., Red, and Boomer
pushed me in a grave
and cranked the casket down
till I was flat, laid out,
my hands above my chest.

"White Boy's learning
how to die,"
they laughed and cried,

then pulled me out
and washed my head.

7
We dug one up instead of down.
The widow came to supervise
the moving to a larger plot.

We winched him high. The vault,
expensive moisture-proof cement,
had split. He tipped
and poured himself a drink.

She knew him right enough.
He rained a putrefaction
you could keep.

8
Each time
the same sad words
for stranger bodies,

women cold with fear,
children weeding noses,

husbands wheezing
rumors of death.

9
I killed a king snake sunning
in the branches of a cedar,
cut him with a spade
until he spilled
his breakfast on the grass.

Five sparrow babies,
slick and sweet,
poured out like heavy jam,
the fruit still warm.

I nudged them in the grave.
The snake, the birds, the man,
together in the ground.

10

When it rains
we bury ourselves
in piles of plastic grass,

in the shed,
with straps and shovels,
and visions of the dead.

11

I don't like to dig
the children's graves.
They cramp you in,
not room enough
to swing your axe
or work a sweat.

I'd like to climb in,
brace my back,
and push them longer.
If I was stronger.

12

"What do you do?"
I build holes in the ground.

Crow Box

"Come with me," my grandfather said,
"We are going to check the crow box."
Then he took me by the hand and we walked
down to where the lane becomes a ravine.
There on a post was a crude little box
and I had to climb three rungs up the fence
to see the yellow chick enclosed.
"But won't it die?" I asked.
"Bait, my son, one life for ten;
each thing in the proper perspective," he said.

Three mornings I carried oats in my pocket,
water in my hand, to check the crow box,
till the black bird was trapped,
its neck wrung like a chicken's.
An old red hen hatched the next chicks,
in safety, behind the catalpa tree,
in the high weeds,
and I took four of her brood
in back of the woodshed
and cut off their heads.

Grandfather Billy

Before he died
his eyes grew dim
from the old explosion.
But he could still see
to feed himself
and to find the steps
before he reached them.
When he would call to us
we would, unmoving,
stand upon the lawn
almost laughing through our fingers
as he passed ten feet away.
And one warm Saturday
he walked to town
with yellow ribbons in his hair.

The Beekeeper's Wife

She wakes beside his body brown as bees.
Why can't he know? She wonders as she waits
why loneliness must be a private thing.
If she could send the messages she keeps
her hands would tell him of her aching bones,
her mouth would be the only sound he knows.
Outside, the queen is dead, the shifting trees
are warm with bees and ripple with the wind
of wings. Oh she would be the keeper's girl
and run with lifted skirts to gather them,
and hang her heart upon a leaf-blown tree
to house them in, and feed them on her blood.

Late Fall, Setting Traps

I climb a fever to the forest.
Coyotes creep by my fingers,
possum hang on my breath.

I enter the tongue of a fox,
the oneness of bees,
my mouth puckering
in persimmon whistles.

Beyond the perimeter of motion
ears blame me into silence,
mistletoe gathers the tops of trees.

I set my traps, the creek
freezing at my step.
I won't catch it next spring
when it gallops like deer down its track.

Passing the Masonic Home for the Aged

Winter has come to the old folks' home.
The summer chairs on the porch
are facing the wall, bending
in prayer. Snow hangs

a shawl across their backs.
On the lawn, weeds grow into drifts,
branches of trees snap
at one another, and do not apologize.

The street has gone away to stay.
Under a roof heavy with clouds
are the faces of ten thousand winters.

Lines on the Ninetieth Birthday of Addie C.

The house grows wild
in a density of vegetation,
vines and trees and rain-turned shingles
brown as the earth,
mounted on the hill:
$\qquad\qquad$ Seventy years:
Invisible and not separate from the land,
but letting its roots coil like the vines
where birds are the same birds
infesting like sweet-voiced rats
$\qquad\qquad$ the deadliness of brown
indistinguishable as the house hiding,
the land's keloid;
Rolling before you the fissured fields,
rivulets of years flown down
$\qquad\qquad$ from the high house,
landscapes of trees grown stiff,
the peach and cherry, the elms diseased,
black walnuts webbed with worms which flower
like fruit to take the morning dew.

2

I picture the young girl.
If beauty is, you were so,
virgin bride in black lace
and formal stance, starched
bones: handsome girl to bear
the land. You bore children,
raised them to yourself
and watched the land destroy.
And then the husband gone,
the young girl dead of his disease,
You were born and reared

to what your children shaped,
and shared in their growth
as you grew thick and wifely
with no husband but the land.

3
I would have known you before,
among the honeysuckle vines,
to touch the bloom, teach and take;
what you were in these young pictures
before you were my blood,
the proud girl in black lace,
a slim life to fashion
in persimmon fields,
                    in love-wound rooms.
I would see our daughter grow
to mother me,
image of you when we met
in vague movements against the sky,
the daughter of you
                    soon taking your desire.
But you are lost to me,
and so is she.
I cry for my mother born
and my mother bearing me.

4
What have you learned?
I never learn, but to adjust.
And now I know you only by your age,
the years you hold to like a walking stick.
The world is older than you ever dreamed:
You've lived to see your sixty-year-old babies die.

Excavations

Kings Canyon, California, 1964

Centuries have passed
since these fires burned in other faces.
Were there lean children in the huts, then,
deer grazing at the edge of the clearing?
Were antelope hides curing in the wind,
pungent and beautiful?
These drawings on the cliff enlighten us.
We notice here their separation from the tribe,
a cruel winter light across high mountains.
And here, the murder of a chief,
the sacrificial burning of his wife.

What do we hope to learn?
We spend our summers here.
There was no great civilization,
no monumental work. They came here, lived,
grew sick, and died. They fed on venison
and squirrel, laid their beds on poplar leaves.
They bound their feet when winter came
and built the snow to keep the wind away.
What decisions did they make?
Where did they miscalculate?
We come with shovels and with sieves
to pan for bones, small hunks of clay, bright beads.

But as we dig we talk of death,
of bodies settling in the ash
of their own fire. And in our tents at night
we gather what we have of what we are,
and learn to wage a kind of love.
The bones collect, the nights grow cold;

we try to resurrect something
from the ashes that we hold.

Picture Puzzle

This piece of sky goes somewhere
above the child's head, the child
with the apple—the sky is blue here,
no clouds in this part of the picture.
But first we must find the child's head.
It is somewhere. We can see the apple,
with the bite missing, in his hand.
But what is this falling like rain?
There are no clouds. Is it tears, or juice
from the apple? We must find the child's head.
He may be hurt. He may need someone
to find his head. And where is the sun?
Let us look for the sun. There are evidences
of it lighting the wings of birds. Somewhere
there must be a sun, and a child's head
with a bite of apple in its mouth.

The Fabulous Frazonis Appear on the Bozo Show

Chicago, 1968

As the curtain parts Pietro is juggling balls,
or heads, or the embryos of chickens
which disappear into his mouth like shy sparrows.
The young sister, Maria, has circled her body
catching her head between her thighs.
She is hoping someone will find this appealing.
Perhaps she will never marry.

Meanwhile, Rodolpho rides the world's smallest bicycle
which gradually disappears into his body. He takes
a double take, then rows off the stage
in an imaginary canoe. The audience howls.

Now the Frazonis are climbing to the sky,
a five-headed caterpillar.
The father shoulders his family.
He seems to be saying his back is strong.
His youngest son vanishes into the rafters
and is not seen again.

The remaining Frazonis drench their bodies
in gasoline for the finale.
Children all over America ignite their Zippos.
Intricate bone structures are revealed
for an instant, like tableaux on the Fourth of July.

Brilliant teeth promenade in rows,
spastic hands curl into smiles.
Bozo is beside himself. He is too much
for himself, and he splinters
into a thousand vibrations on the laugh-o-meter.

For a Woman Whose Fiancé Was Killed at War

The war has entered you like a lover
Such a flowering there inside you

You are big with war blossoming
You have swallowed the war
The still nights of your body rising in walls.

The war cradled in you cannot get out
It is there and there and there

And your eyes are bees your eyes are watching
The war blooming within you.

I have seen such blossoming:
The oriental games of paper flowers
In the instant of birth becoming bright.

Your eyes are such flowers
The war has reached your eyes your eyes have flowered
And fearful are the flowers of your eyes.

The war has filled you with its dead
You are becoming the war

You are becoming the dead rising within you
And fearful are the colors of the dead.

We will bury you between the pages of a book.
We will bury the image you leave.
We will forget your fragrance.

Winter in a Different House

We are beginning to discover
the sounds that break our sleep,
which rooms house winds
that blow from nowhere known.
Last night I felt snow
seep into my face,
and listened to the furnace
try to right itself.
By morning, ice glittered
in our eyes,
the children were gone,
perhaps into cupboards
where they hang like mugs,
and birds were napping
in the fireplace,
waiting to be born.
I searched for kindling.
Now we fix our breakfast.
Toast smolders on the grill.
We eat our daily lives.

Spring Commences

It is like winter
although the children wade
in mud ponds
and flowers float like birds
across the field.
Winter has been here.
One can see that. Your face
is of winter. I noticed this
before, in that landscape,
after the deep snow,
reflections of coldness,
of clear sky,
before the earth broke through.
The coldness remains
although your hand
turns the fresh soil,
and insects disembark
like explorers from canoes
to search the dark land.

The Drinkers

In this morning light
I think how you seem like my father,
your head skulled on the table
like a bowling ball.
And once in the night
I thought it was a driftwood planter,
pale cactus flowers
blooming from its eyes,
and I thought the movement was an ant.
Old friend, how do you live,
taking no food,
and the wine tasting of salt?
How do you hold on
and every morning bare those wintered gums
to pull another gusher from the jug
and call my name?

Julius Caesar Appears on a Late-Night Talk Show

"Are you something of yourself as Julius Caesar?"
—a question from the audience

Something, yes. I used to be more
but liked it less. I recall
I was a masochistic fry cook
from Whittier, my arms done
up to the elbows. I love good crisp skin.
I burned like a self-destruct message.

And once I entered from outer space,
the rage that week,
but someone fiddled with my hatch
and I couldn't get back.

You may remember the queer chemist
with a new formula for living.
You begin by shaving your legs.
Or the time I came as a national crisis.
I tightened your belts, didn't I?
You thought I was playing games.
I was dead serious.

But enough of this. I could go on
telling you lies, and you would believe me.
I am something of myself,
but no natural child. I am a zoo.
I am for all the world like you
taking root in the corner of your set.
Listen to me. Quit plotting my suicide.
My people, give me a chance.

The Derelict

How fine it is
to wet one's pants,
the sudden warmth
burning like a dream.

How can I explain?

This wine is my family.
I give birth to children
in my bones, their
snug voices singing
to my fingers and my toes.

But one must often let go
of what is best in life.
I grow cold inside.

Goodbye, my children.
You die down my legs,
waking me to your going.

The Watcher

In the near dark of my mind,
shadows of breasts,
of hands undoing.
I imagine disheveled beds,
a loosening of legs,
that dank, pure spot:
the totems of my faith.
Above me, always,
windows glisten like stars.
I climb the stairs.
A woman, frayed and bare,
comes into the room.
She darkens my sight.
I press too close,
shining in the night.
Across the room
we touch. We feel
our deaths commute
a terrible distance.

The Astronaut

At first I think of my wife,
the way she drank my body in a toast
then said goodbye, the letting go;
of that deep pool where I dove for children.
I believed I saw my children
standing in the yard; then countries,
continents, all of Earth.
Now nothing minute is defined.
I am no poet. I have lost Earth.
I think of how it looks like nothing
but a child's painted ball.

Someone imagined me in this universe;
I invent nothing: I open doors, and it is there.
From here I see a spinning disc
that turns my mind,
dark as the soul of matter,
as it plows across fields of space,
and I cannot remember that grave world,
the pull of love, the purge of war.
I could not dream mankind.
In this madhouse womb all is new.
I could not imagine even you.

The Burial Queen

For Mrs. Emma Smith of Skegness, who holds the world's record for being buried alive — 100 days, ending September 17, 1968, at Raven's Head, Nottinghamshire, England

1
Cameras
memorize
my face.

The earth
answers
all questions.

2
It is difficult
to live
with one's self.

Everything
is first
person.

3
My eyes
darken
with time

My ears
silent
as mushrooms

My thoughts
in braille.

4
These hands
comfort my body

feeding
like delicate
deer.

How lonely
I would be
without them!

5
Memory
drowns
in darkness.

I try
to imagine
the sun.

6
Maggots
climb
my face.

Do I carry
their seed
in my flesh?

7
What went wrong?
What am I
doing here?

And So Forth . . .

When I lost my mind
seven health inspectors in silk ties
entered my head.
They liked what they saw and they said:
"This head will do."
But it didn't.

When I lost my mind
seven slum landlords in disguise
entered my head.
They liked what they saw and they said:
"This head will rent."
And it did.

Moving Out

How do you tell your body goodbye?
If there is much of it, do you miss it more?
Do you say, Look here,
we've had enough of one another.
When I get home tonight
you had best be gone.
Will this work?
Would it be better to leave while sleeping,
a note planted on the pillow like a kiss?
I have known those who favor delusions,
or who forget to bring their bodies home
from work, who reappear in strange cities
        with new faces.
But it is hard to fool those eyes
opening your mirror each morning.
Can you lose your body in an ocean?
Will it really dissolve in tears?
My grandmother told hers goodbye, slowly,
pound by pound, until she had found
a young girl, lost for years in the deepest mountains.
And I have changed my body several times,
that I remember. But each old corpse comes washing back.
And I am running out of trunks, and closets,
and family names, and all my disguises.

from *Sleeping Woman*, 2005

I.

Sleeping Woman

after the painting by Richard Diebenkorn

I'm walking east down Lovell in Kalamazoo
in the middle of the afternoon, and it's hot, July
something, and there's a man sleeping on the sidewalk—
the way you would in your bed—his body a kind of Z
in a fancy serif font, the curlicue of hands
beneath his head at the top, and the toes of each foot
curved to comfort the other, at the bottom. At first
I don't know if he's alive or dead, his skin
the color of burnt iron, a darkness alcohol finally brings.
I remember him from months before, a couple of blocks
west of here. He leaned against my car and wanted
to borrow money, a loan. He wanted a ride to South Haven
where he could get the money to pay me back.
His voice had that desperate familiarity that says:
You know me. You must want to care for me.
I think I gave him something, not much, and drove away.
I couldn't forget his face, murky with solitude,
like the hard red clay in Oklahoma where I grew up
that won't grow anything—everything lost to erosion
that brings such desolation you can't survive.
I thought he wouldn't survive more than a week or so,
but here he is, and when the cops arrive they know him,
call him Billy, and he's still alive, maybe
for the last time, and they pick him up.
I head east again, turn left into the cool museum
where I lose myself, sometimes, where I find you
sleeping where I've seen you before, paint streaming
around you like water, gathering in the shallows
of your dress. I am always surprised to see you.
I don't know. Are you flesh, or water? If I move
you will disappear in a startle of color.

The gallery is almost dark—those new-fangled spots
that keep the viewer anonymous—but your face turns
toward me from the crook of your doubled arms,
all about you an unencumbered sway, an intelligence
of light explicit as a summer evening. Deer quietly chewing.
I balance, in the shadows, between.

The Unforgiven

It is strange
how sometimes
no matter
if we live for years
a good and loving life
we are never forgiven
our smallest transgressions

those first wavering steps
in the wrong direction
never to be brought back

although we stand
in the unlit doorway
late into the darkness
calling down
the narrow
and otherwise
empty street.

Mime

That feeling of someone there
so she turns to peer over her shoulder
but the sidewalk clicks empty
and no one at the open window she passes.
Still, that unease, like the distress
of curtains settling, the failing lung of air
as she turns again, and, oh, there is
someone, someone familiar,
as if she has stepped aside
and sees herself as she might be.
It must be one of those street mimes,
one of those who gather a living
becoming what one cannot become,
becoming her walk, her grace
and particularity, her flesh
as it furls and dips, playing
to those who watch just out of reach,
with a smirk, with shoulders winking,
arms straight at the sides
but the hands tipped outward,
spilling the cooled tea;
so that as she turns
there is only that figure turning
in pirouette, its skirt wheeling
in the brilliant silk of motion, the face
already lost in the unaccountable distance.

In a Field of Sunlight

We will walk into the field
of goldenrod splintered
by the sun's foolishness.
We have been there before,
after a rain,
when the water streamed
like the grain of wood
around obliterations
of limb, and knots
of mourners recalling
other losses, other rains.

The mind as it chills
returns to sunlight
and the child's leaping stitch
across the field,
bobbing above weeds
and remorse, until we go
to meet her
where she progresses,
where she rises
into the arms' reach,
her gnatty hair gleaming.

Nude on a Kitchen Stool

Knee up, herself
apart from the air

her flesh dispenses
its own revolutions

intersecting moons.
Not a train on a siding

or a spoon banging
a tin pie plate

but a moon dividing
her body in porcelain blooms.

Bees

The bees found an entrance below
the eavestrough, a passage
where the stucco gaped an invitation
early last fall, too late,
I would think, to establish
winter store. Their business
kept me away from overflowing
leaves wedging drains,
so that autumn rains brewed
and rose and fell
into window wells two stories below.
And I with no courage or will
to force their fury
let them build and save
until winter closed the door,
then bought the poison to apply.
With ladder, spray, and caulk
I sealed them in their vault and thought:
this is the last of it. But in the nights
that followed, that turned to months,
in that dark house I listened
to their darkness, their blind assault
that seemed like sleet within the walls,
those starved, bony bees chalking
their maze, marking blind alleys
again and again, until I longed
for any way to wrench them loose,
set them free, stop their ticking.
When would they settle, give in,
begin to write their pleas
for forgiveness, their wills?
With what mute remonstrance
would they inhabit
that numb peace before drowning?

November

It is raining today, the slick
whale backs of sidewalks
surfacing along the block.
Look how the earth throws them
up, buckled, breaking. The fallen
leaves, raked into humps, flatten,
press down like hands.
If I were to reach my hand
into the rich, wet leaves
and lift them to my face, I would smell
the season's blood, animal, insect,
the evidence of earthly living.
Each thing has left its mark, its scent,
all the ravelled fragments of birth
and death fallen into place.
North of here, November glistens, a new
snow sticking to everything: branches
of trees, cats curled on porches, the
steaming backs of horses. Distance turning
rain to snow or snow to rain. Each
is pain and beauty, wet pavement glowing
in the pale November noon, or snow its own
illumination, each winding across time
and distance a dark path.

Neighbor

For years he has tilled his yard,
his wife and two children
the fruit of his labor, a dog
behind the chain-link fence.
We are cordial: Yes, we must get together.
We nod, his wife nods.
As I drive by
on my way to work he waves
like a friendly guard at the border.
Once I saw eighteen canoes stacked
in his yard. A scouting trip
up north, I think. Twice
he was operated on for cancer.
I know little else about him.
We are set apart like our two houses.
And today, seeing him in his yard
for the thousandth time, raking leaves,
red hunting jacket ablaze in the autumn light,
his dark-browed face bent to his task,
I felt a sudden snap,
as if something had closed
for the last time. It felt
involuntary as a swallow,
something that quick and ordinary,
and I knew an irretrievable distance.
I would never lie down beside him,
drunk with wine and silence.
I would never take his wife into my arms,
saying *sorry, sorry.*

And the Sleet Cometh Down

i.

Her skull a white stone
flower set in a slender vase,
her face, the planes
of forehead and cheek, the apple
of her chin, unadorned by skin
or color. I would lay my hand
across the formal brow, feel
the cold, curved bone taking
my skin and flesh until nothing
remains but bone upon bone.
And the caves of her eyes,
if there are eyes,
cheeks, even without flesh, curved
and high, and the only color
a thick red wrist of hair
plaited down the back
of the skull, laid carelessly across
the front of her left shoulder.

ii.

A tug on the river
makes a mosaic of ice
after the winter storm
warning us into our own
warm bodies, the prow plotting
the ice into new design,
a mortar of water sealing
the passage, as the final breath
hazes the glass where one finger
could pulse a new channel,
like a tug whose whistle
heard from this room

resounds between memory
and what is.

The Most Terrible and Beautiful Thing

The earth opening, bodies startled
from their graves, lungs like butterflies.
Hearts like matches striking

catch, take hold, not all
at once, but each in its own dark time.
"Is this the moment we were promised?"

They touch each other like the blind.
The past is future, the future closed
forever in the past. Each thing returns

to its beginning, crops to the fields, pasture
to woods, rivers clear to pure thin tongues.
Machines are put to sleep like toothless dogs.

The assassin sips his breakfast coffee
robbed of purpose. Rain climbs
the morning sky. At first, a blessing,

the dead in the arms of their loved ones.
And yet, these poor souls, how mystified
and fierce to see their lives erased,

to know the certain term of infancy,
the seed unspent as fathers steal them
from their earthly home.

How bitter is that death called birth
as our brief time begins, is spent,
and God will not relent.

II.

Conversation

"A bird is hiding in your head.
It is opening its wings to soar."

"Yes, but like a hanged man."

The Song the Stone Child Sings

In her womb I turned,
and stroked, and sucked
my dinner down.
I never woke
to a world I did not know.
Face half-finished,
head bent, eyes closed:
which god did I kneel to?

I think it is the god
of silence, the god
of eternal darkness.
Unnamed, I named myself.
I am a small stone
in the womb of love
and I will thrive
after all flesh dies.

Wolf

Gnaw of flesh, skin and tendon cleaving,
furred moons wet as newborn pups.
And the howl of limbs, eyes splintering
light, tongue a body of its own making,
licking clean after, nothing left
but the bone of darkness sucked bright.

The Song the Burnt Child Sings

I have no lips, no nose,
my mouth is a howl,
my tongue a choir.
No one can clap my ears.

I can bite.

Must I thank God for my eyes?
They will not close.
The world spills ceaselessly into them.

If I could have hair or ears,
or nose, or eyes that close,
which would I choose?
None of those.

Lord, give me lips to kiss this life.

Question

The children in her veins are awake now
though they slept awhile ago. They turn
slowly, as one does while waking, and press
their small, blue faces against her skin.
What can they see through this yeasty screen?
The earth of trees, rock, sky? We can see
the slow pulse of their mouths, the exhalation
of dreams. Will they come out, will they
trust air? Or will they nod to sleep again
curled up in the blood's dark lair?

The Song the Suicide Sings

Let the trees still spend their elaborate gestures,
   the air give evidence.
It is good to be home for the last time.
All the comforts of comfort.
The hum, the thousand parts,
a marvel of production, assembly.
Dear ones, my heartland, my oath,
the crime of my crime.
I float, a flower on water.
I hunger for its hunger,
the sweet digestion, the dark
dependency of want. I smell
my death. A miraculous silence.
I can hear the stars breaking.

Mendelssohn at Midnight

Unmerciful music.

The brassy stars are immune.

It is flesh that burns in the pure dark.

The Father's Song

Make me a father, the child says.

The city is a fallen leaf
and I am father of the city,
father of the broken window,
father of distance, father of blight.

Child, spooned into your skin,
give me the faint nape hair
that bends to my breath, give me
the small beginnings of words,

the vowels opening like hands;
give me your hands, your fingers
empty of rings, give me back
language, give me back sorrow.

Words lie down in the grass
like beautiful insects
in their own alien world,
like women in their giving.

And I am father of light, father
of lucid meadows, father of
returnings. I am father
of the blue-veined cock,
father of seed, father of dying.

Games

At dusk the children enter
the tall grass of evening.
They play games with their bodies.
They are looking for something
that is not there, not in the shadows
of their eyes. If I were to ask them
Whose children are you, they would
touch my face with their open mouths
and eat the flesh of my black tears.

The Mother's Last Song

Child, you do not sing
the toad's song
in the iris weeds.

You do not capture fire
in your mouth. You do not
unwind your slithery arms.

In the night of the long grass,
in the night of the black sky,
no flurry of stars.

You are the memory
of your beginning,
another ice age.

In you we find our perfect grave,
the soul pure and rising,
the sea caught in clerical stillness.

She Dreams a Letter from Her Son

Mother, don't hide your dreams in my head.
Mother, my eyes haven't opened yet.
Mother, the days are puppies put to sleep.

Mother, the cottonwoods are crying in the night.
Mother, I am too young to go to school.
Mother, you touched my face and lost your fingers there.

Mother, a gun is a good teacher.
Mother, I have learned my lesson.
Mother, I am staying after school.

The Song the Old Woman Sings

These children are not mine.
When the woman selling tamales comes by
I say to her, *I am a spinster.*
But my belly tells on me.
An ancient face that knows too much,
it stares at me until I turn away.

Why must babies suck beauty from one's breasts?
Fat little ticks, they won't let go
until one's body has closed all its shops
of candles and incense and sweet-smelling soaps.

Yesterday I caught the wrong bus home.
Late, I ran alongside, shouting, beating the door.
The driver let me in. But it was a bus
of children on their way to a museum,
and I sat by their teacher, bewildered
for a moment, afraid
all those faces had found me out.

The Air We Now Breathe

This air is part of the blood
of those who are now dead.
It rises from the grass like sunlight.
Now it enters the lungs of those who survive,
of the children, of the haltered soldiers
where particles of death are filtered to fall
helplessly to the earth, like bodies,
like seeds that will not take root.

The Song the Minister Sings

I am like a woman with two loves.
I would not lie to God.
Will I say the right name?

The old men in libraries read the news for warmth.
When will their names rise up and not their bodies?

Yesterday I prayed for a young man
shrunk to the size of his bones:

Pain, your apron is full.
Thrust that bitter fruit
down his throat. Choke him.

It is the same each day.
I see the children in busses
making tongues and crossed eyes
against the world, laughing at God.

Winter Day

Up here, where our hearts thrive
and our bones burn like logs
it is warm. But our feet know
the coldness of death, the invisible
slain fallen in the snow.
There have been many lost.
We cannot see the bodies
as we step carefully among them.

The Song the Lost Children Sing

The sun is breaking bottles in our eyes.

We are those whose names you do not know
who lift your blood through our hearts.

Are you afraid?

On the shore we sift through your fingers
trying to get back to first things.

We enter the ocean to heal our wounds.
Someone says we are somewhere beyond
the earth's curve, in the whales' cave,
our hands holding nothing but themselves.

We are lanterns lost at sea. There is no help for us.
We are burning into something immortal.
You will discover our names in the houses of fish.

Rain After Midnight

The new widow is walking

barefoot on wooden floors

through the early morning hours.

The Song the Assassin Sings

The knife is a prayer
the flesh answers.

Kneel, an old woman
planting tulips.
I come to bless you.

The isolation
is so beautiful.

To live outside,
to be an alien
in this skin,

to be perfect
beyond your belief.

If there were some other
god I would know him.

Bedtime Story

The fledgling earth
awoke one morning.
The egg had cracked
and the sun settled
her skirts about him
to keep him warm.
The sky blinked
and the earth peeped
in a most endearing
fashion. The sun
nurtured him
until he grew fat
and toddled, a tagalong,
behind her. And she
said, You are a bright boy
and when you grow up
I hope your own children
will be as lovely as you.
And she warmed his feathers
with the flame of her hand.
As the story goes,
he grew, a handsome fellow,
and fathered many children,
mostly beautiful, and some
lived, and some died,
and some broke his heart . . .
"Is there no end to this story?"

III.

My Father's Fortune

Silence was my father's fortune,
carried with him everywhere for safekeeping,
houses and cars and offices crowded with silence.
And trailing my father

four fair-skinned children of different sizes,
a matched set of luggage,
silence folded inside like Sunday clothes.
Everything my father owned transporting silence.

But not a silence of anger or isolation.
Instead, one of yearning, inarticulate
and fumbling. A silence that learned
its own language, its own stubborn love.

Mother at the Mirror, 1939

She says
her lean evening
prayers
for the flesh
fingers dipped
in Pond's
cold cream
blessing
her face
before the bird's-eye
maple dresser
children tucked
asleep
beneath the rim
of wind-whipped
sheets.

Oklahoma Pastoral

The woman snapping beans
from the oak rocker on the east porch
is the one I would marry,
but I am only four, sitting at her feet,
a fly swatter across my lap.

Now I see her rise.
Her chair begins to sing
its own diminished song,
her skirts drift by, winging my face.

I climb from the floor, follow,
swinging the fly swatter, back and forth,
innocent in the buzzing air.

My Father's Bulldogs

i.

My father bred bulldogs on Pickard Street.
Our neighbors learned to hate us.
As many as a dozen animals growling and barking.
Misshapen dwarf-dogs, tongues askew,
flies boiling from excrement.

And vicious locked battles in the street.
My father at work.
My mother and my older sisters prying jaws apart
with brooms and mop handles.

Later, exhausted brutes wheezing and moaning.
Crodie, the family pet,
on the back porch, vomiting
behind the wicker clothes hamper.

ii.

One night someone slipped into our garage
to tap in the heads of a new litter with a hammer.
Like a cook cracks eggs.

You always think you know who does something like that.
The unemployed brothers who lived across the street
and down with their mother, next door to the house
of the young girl bitten by a black widow spider.

iii.

My father brushed the bulldogs' coats for hours,
his quiet Saturday ritual,
trimmed their thick toenails,
taped their ears into roses.
As if *any* human labor could make them beautiful.

I loved Albert Payson Terhune whose dogs were sleek
and lovely, collies with finely tuned heads
who moved like thoroughbred horses. Or dogs
who were half-wild, fathered by wolves,
who became civilized for the love of a human.

iv.

My younger sister, Addie, buried Crodie (alive) in her sandbox,
trimmed his ears with blunt-nosed paper scissors.
(Crodie wincing ever-so-slightly, apologetically.)

It was my fault Crodie killed our Easter chickens.
I left their shoebox in the back yard.
My sisters, forgiving, let me attend the funeral.

v.

In my room, perched on the edge of the bed,
my mother and father, embarrassed, in straight chairs,
doors closed on older sisters, I failed
What Every Young Boy Should Know.

So my father, shy in sexual matters,
took me to the garage
to watch him breed the bulldogs.

Those hushed evenings, my father's arms
around the bitch holding her steady
as Crodie circled, coughing, sniffing,
until his cock hung slick and limber.

My father, finally, taking the pendulous cock in his hand
to work it in before the fist-sized knot could form.
Crodie's soft black jowls leaking a satisfied drool.

vi.

Driving to dog shows late at night with my father
through Oklahoma, Kansas, Missouri, the wing
windows of the Pontiac cranked open,
a stream of air across our faces,
ice-cold Coca-Colas from late-night diners
or vending boxes at filling stations.

Riding in silence through the dark passage of country,
smelling the languid, unclothed land, pungent,
like the body at night, opening, the held heat rising.

Marshmallows

One week I gave Curtiss Saf-T-Pops to every girl
on Pickard Street for kisses, and Mary Lynn,
who loved me best, slapped my face
for no good reason. That week, Maurice broke
his arm falling from the peach tree
onto a pile of flagstones that would never be our patio.
On Saturday we three piled twigs and small branches,
roasted wieners until they curled and split
on the crusted grill. I whittled
poplar branches for marshmallows. Mary Lynn's
were brown and tender as swollen thumbs.
Mine blazed into blackened crusts.
Maurice grew himself a charcoal mustache.
Errol Flynn, wounded hero, home from the war.
"Oh, that? It's nothing. Only a scratch."
Mary Lynn laughed and her green eyes flared
brighter than fireflies. We lay down
on the navy blanket my father sent home
from the Canal Zone and listened to voices
from neighboring houses, the occasional chatter of cars.
Mary Lynn had to go home but Maurice stayed.
I think she loved us both that night.
We heard her singing down the alley,
the creak and slam of her screen door,
and felt too strange to speak.

Evening Dawn

for Sue

I remember an evening on the farm,
my sister and I on the lawn after rain,
young foxes in a green pasture,
the sun gone behind miles of clouds
and the western sky black;

yet a strange green light over all,
crickets sounding in the trees,
leaves like tongues spilling wetness,
the damp breath of their singing;

and my sister and I on the lawn
listening to quail calling,
the evening holding light like the sea,
the sun lost in the deeps of the sky;

yet as if by miracle
a light coming from the east,
from a clear sky beyond massed clouds:
an evening dawn, sending shadows westward;

and we stood in that luminous gift,
in that moment out of order
as if the earth had turned a new orbit,
our lives long shadows before us.

Hearts

"I prefer the dark meat," Mother says,
"so much more flavorful."

"Moist, delicious," Grandmother says.

Father and Grandfather love breast and wishbone.

"Brother loves the heart,"
these women croon, my sisters, too.

Chicken heart, goose heart, duck heart, turkey heart.

"Come to the kitchen, Brother,
your heart is ready!"

Oh, steamy heart gleaming on a white plate.
Jewel, crown, mouthful of joy—
how they sing its praises!

And I, most favored of boys,
come to that warm, stirred room
and chew the heart down.

Farm Dogs

On the farm there were always dogs,
mostly mongrels, shabby brindle,
spotted, or off-white, abandoned
by townspeople, finding their way
up the lane to our house, finding
their way into my heart
through unswerving devotions, companions
of the fields, loafers in the kafir corn
or oats while I mended fence
or worked the posthole digger,
dogs thankful for scraps from supper,
eaters of rabbits, mice from the corn crib,
incessant bearers of pups wedged like potatoes
in the far recesses of the cellar, dogs grateful
not to be kicked or beaten, to be tolerated,
never having slept under a roof,
curled at the foot of a bed, grateful
not to be shot for sport by hunters
or irate farmers, dogs who looked you in the eye,
tongues heavy with happiness.

That Summer

That summer nothing would do
but we sink the boat
in the heart of the lake
and swim in the cool night
for the yellow fire on the beach.

Through the dark water.

We all made it but Ronald,
whom we never found,
who was never Ronald
again; each fish I catch
since, I ask *Ron, is that you?*

The Death and Resurrection of Jesse James

d. April 3, 1882, St. Joseph, Missouri

Oh, the dirty little coward
Who shot Mr. Howard
And laid poor Jesse in his grave

God Bless Our Home
the framed sign
you were straightening
when Bob Ford shot you.
What pitiful desire
I imagine, Zerelda
tapping the nail
into the plaster wall,
near where the bullet
would later flatten,
on Christmas Eve, in 1881,
moving into this strange house
with two small children
and you, Mr. Howard,
a cattle buyer down
on his luck.
You were nearly broke.

Why do I come here
and pay my dollar?
To see brother Frank's
rattlesnake necktie
and stickpin, the pictures
of little Mary and Jesse Edward?
I don't know. Sometimes
the past is more poignant
than we suppose. You were

cruel and crazy, at best.
Yet your tough old mother
sacrificed one leg
to a Pinkerton bomb
thrown through her window
for you, and survived
three husbands and one son.

Jesse, they made your flesh new
sixty and seventy years later,
old, grizzled men wetting
their lips in nursing homes
across the western states
claiming your name, your birth,
but not your death
in that small room.
The escape . . . yes!
The miraculous escape
and the honest life
lived in the shadow
of your legend.
Until, come to this,
it was time to confess,
to embrace whatever honor
the world bestows upon
its dead and risen angels.

I grew up in Oklahoma,
loving your name
and the bearded faces
on the front pages
of slow news days
of the Norman *Transcript*
and the Guthrie *Daily Leader*
wanting them to be
true resurrections.

Wouldn't that be lovely,
if our lives could be reclaimed?
At the auction
after your death
your daughter's high chair
sold for seventy-five cents.
The family dog, the star
of this occasion, was good
for fifteen dollars.
And you? A hero
worthy only of burial space
and intermittent memories
for the brief duration
of two small hearts.

Evening, Milking

Each day redeemed by evening.

The stammering sunset.
The moon in its rut of sky.

The mind is white wicker.

Cows, heavy with the business of milk,
nod home from the east pasture.

There is a moan that milk makes.

The clatter of hooves, the lovely cow eyes.
Thrown oats. The rasp of rough tongues.

My grandmother's small hands.

It is true the earth cries out at dusk.
Its various voices.

To Death, For My Father

Death, this man
is dancing. See
how you can't see
his moves, so quick
his feints confuse,
counter your low
illicit hay-maker
harvesting air, nothing,
which makes you
appear foolish
as he bends double
with sputtering laughter,
and you swing
again, over his head,
losing balance, falling,
surprised at his face
twisted above you, counting.

St. Petersburg, My Father Walks the Beach

Each slow
foot

a lever
lifted

an empty
cylinder

clicked

Poem

The voices of the dead,
how they come back to us,
like apples in summer . . .

Rocking on the east porch
in the shade of chinese elm,
black walnut, iced tea and hot
apple pie, red-skin cheese,
flies itching on the screen . . .

My grandmother's voice
rising above the piano
in the parlor,
Dearie, my dearie, long summer days
have drifted away . . .

The voices of the dead,
they surface
like the heads of swans . . .

IV.

Snowstorm on Mozart's Birthday

Kalamazoo, Michigan

The teachers of winter
let down their long hair.

We lie back on our beds
and disappear
in the pale, quiet muslin.

Twenty-seven inches of snow,
and Mozart on the radio.

The neighbors are pushing
through five-foot swells of snow.
Where will they go?

The city is adrift,
but Mozart on the radio.

Mozart, we are thankful.
The air glistens with music
and we lie back again and again.

The sky flings down its lovely notes.
Mozart on the radio.

The Blue Turtle

We cup our hands
against distance, build

a lean-to of knuckles,
kindle a small flame

in the palm of space.
What we own, what we carry.

It is only in the blood-beating
tick of our hearts

against the almost human
whistle of winter

the small blue turtle
each day makes up

a new world, disordered
and reckless, of surprises.

In the Palm of Space

"The wishing heart of you I loved, Kalamazoo"
—*Carl Sandburg*

i.

Infinite is the string
that pulls the darkness out,
turns a pocket into daylight,

an ear of moon
listening to the earth
above the long horizon.

The houses of the city
flush with desire,
each window a sunrise.

ii.

Someone is waking, her face
at the window, a woman
in a pink slip beckoning.

Will it avail us not to go?

Will we remember
her familiar gestures,
her words already spoken?

She leans one hand
on the bird's-eye dresser,
hip slung in the warm glint

of her slip, her body
the sleeve we touch,
longingly, in a crowd.

iii.

When evening comes
and the air is blue and kindly,
she rubs her hands for warmth,
the small fire spitting
from crumpled paper and kindling
sparks like hyphens.

Distance is always there,
in the crevices of speech,
in the cramped quarters
of the moon. She thinks the moon
is a mouth, a smile or a cry
we disregard, trying to keep
the blood in. We don't want
out, we want in. The chains
around our shoulders, the hulls
of sleep, her head nestled in the pit
of his arm circling her body,
the rope she dangles from.

Climb out or climb in,
don't fall, a stone
down mountain slopes,
your neck bending, graceful
as a wrist, hesitant
clouds of breath like dust
rising and settling, your face,
the head thrown back, suddenness
of desire, toppled, the bite of earth.

iv.

A man is walking his dog,
the snow falling in thick clusters,
small, fat fists of snow. The dog
shakes her coat, a flurry

of fleas dislodged, a game
of blind man's bluff.
The bandage removed,
the eyes have disappeared.

How strange to be alone,
someone's children crying
from their beds,

little large-eyed owls.
A dumb show
of trees against the sky.

Wood explodes as it dies,
the ring of years released
in flame and smoke,
as when the mind goes.

Our bodies in drifts,
tinder for the fire.

Ten degrees, wet muzzles
paint the windows. Inside,
a woman sleeps, her hand pale and open
like an empty eye socket.

v.
She has been closed, now,
for some months,
like a room after a death.
The bed has been made
with clean sheets.
But no one sleeps there.

In the garden she sees
her face in the cabbage

still growing from the earth,
its thick white root. She twists
with two hands cupped
over the ears, no Mozart,
no Schubert, snaps the head loose,
carries it on her hip, in the crook
of her arm, like a child
needing to be spanked. She sets it
on the kitchen table, her mother's
table, oak and scars, old wax
and varnish, where it rocks
in its chair and is no longer her face.

The worms come,
an onslaught of commas,
disconnected phrases, leaves
falling like words, not praising
the air or the earth, finding fault,
the tree caught in a web
of its own making,
worms smirking in the drift
of their silken parachutes,
ribbed leaves shot through,
ventricles of air sobbing,
the worms hanging
like sacks of hearts
sucking up all the blood,
embryos curbed and feeding.
Her tree, its fruit hard green polyps
strewn, splitting, blackening.

vi.
The corpse of a barn lies
in a heap on the black soil.
You see others in Michigan,
Oklahoma, perhaps anywhere

in this country, gone too far,
a terminal illness. The old lady
dead, what's the use? Who's to plant
flowers, paint the mailbox?
So it's left to rot,
a slow corpse, perhaps
twenty years to collapse
into the earth. Is the smell
in the wood, the rot,
the angle of boards?

vii.
Lie with me, old woman,
in the river's murky bed,
in the fellowship of water.

The morning fog,
eddies of morning fog.

Black-and-white cows
standing in the stilled water,
drinking deeply, tails singing,
the old motion, the same story.
Two on the river bank under
a tree, six in the water, udder deep.

Let me kneel in the thick mud,
take the swarthy, warted teats
in my hands. The mooing river.

viii.
The woman with two husbands hangs
sheets on the line. Will they dry
in time? Her hands are sparrows
on her thighs. She prepares:
How will it be? She sweetens

her body. One man turns the corner
of her mouth. She tastes him.
She practices the other's name.
One loves her fallen breasts,
the long nipples naming
the earth, the way she falls back
into the caves of the bed, her body
parting like a loaf of bread.

One palms the sun,
slips it into his pocket.
He's keeping it for her hair.

ix.
She doesn't want to lie down
among strangers, their buttocks
stiffening into shell,
two skulls beneath her palms.
They lower above her
like the sun coming down,
for a moment the reddest sky
she has ever seen.

In this cascade of noons
and loosened ties, of afternoons
spilled from the torn pockets
of travelers, of disembodied words,
motes in air shafts, sunlight drifting
pellucid snow, this is you
knowing your life is more
than you can ever earn, this
is you in the distant shadows
watching yourself so tangible
in sleep, as if you could
reach out and touch your life.

x.

Beneath the ice, in February,
something frozen awaits
the hiss of yesses, spins
in the cold bark of wings.
Leaves sigh like children asleep,
the earth questions winter.

A man and a woman are walking
in a marsh. She touches him.
His skin clings to her fingers
everywhere she turns.

xi.

Is there a death we experience after death?
The eyes of rocks glinting through centuries.

The tumble of stars.

We lie back in the sweet grass,
spent and out of breath.

Our mouthless speech is such
we imagine the dead would know.

We sleep. Among all those voices.

xii.

Someone is mowing after dark.

The path is a fresh, damp
green, the mad cylinder

whirling, shooting up
little sparks of grass.
It must hurt those trees

to be so green. The sky
riffling its feathers, the earth
a nest of twigs and string,
a few bottle caps. If we could understand
the day's dear gibberish
we would ring its tin cup with coin.

xiii.
The sunlight must be said,
the way it sings
as it strolls across the city,
hands in its pockets.
And the clean laundry of clouds.
We must say how we slip
into these clothes
as if our bodies were
transparent as vowels.

Her yeasty breasts wet and warm,
and he comes, lovely fish,
mysterious breather, climbing
from the ocean, taking hold
of air, lungs unfurling. She
catches him in her two hands,
wet weather, gull cry, turtle crawl.

Painted Lady. Pearly
Eye. Mourning Cloak.
The sun has learned
to touch the wings open.
They swell, divide like lips.
Salves of birth smooth their entry,
the giving way and the giving.
This world where flight is possible.

xiv.

The girl lugging her satchel of surprises
to school may give them up,
one by one, until
she is empty of desire.
Today, a blackbird would flip
out, unzipped, a word
sleeping on its tongue,
the word we hunger for.

Our children may rise to new life
if we give birth, breath, name,
to that which yet may live.

xv.

Call the children in,
supper on the table.
Dusk, a skitter of starlings
in the ravine, skateboards
on the pavement.
A woman rakes leaves
along the width of her yard,
her small hands placed
so and so on the long handle
of the rake, a sinewy strength
in her arms, in the fury
of her labor, the wheel of leaves
flung into the air, spinning,
climbing, a froth of leaves
like water set into motion
by the tide of her body,
everything caught up
in the undertow,
twigs, stones,
dirt, until
the woman—laughing, crying—

leaps deeply into that surf,
drowning, rising up.

xvi.
We will be late in traffic.

Glasses shed frost
on the marble counter.

Above the mirror
time tells its usual story.

And then in the moon
of the wakened flesh
we listen to the lisp
of our bodies, delicate
as light the tongue sheds,
delicate as the crevices of mica,
as her voice saying
there, there, there,
and the nose is an animal
burrowing, a snail
shell, a house at dusk
where a woman without thinking
wipes her palms on
the curve of her hips,
spoons heaped with dessert.

Small fragments of rescue.

The hand, no matter
how crippled, how betrayed
saved by the warmth
of blessed skin and flesh.
No comfort like this,
burning and burning, tender
and tentative recognitions.

xvii.

Kalamazoo, you are wealthy
with spring. The shelves
of your trees are stocked
with green. I can hear the hidden
discourse. The momentary
whirlpools of leaves.
The grass is deep, unmowed.
Too late.
The dandelions have scattered
their million seeds.

The fur that pearls the underside
of leaves, the down on upper
lip, the purse of cheek bone,
lobe of ear, the way a blossom
furls, unfurls. Sweet intercourse,
the moisture's tongue
taking its curl of honey,
the rub and welt of taste.

xviii.

Is this the day we save ourselves?

The earth welcomes us
into the shuddering dark.

Let the dirt clean and shine
our hearts, let us peel
to the pure cave of the soul.

Mother night, shake out the stars.

Poem

for Shirley

Isn't it here
in the unnamed
giving of light,
bodies of earth and water
lifted and taken
into the orbit of flesh;
isn't it the waking
of blood and bone
to another earthly presence
moving across the space
of a lighted window
as though it were
the universe;
isn't it the breaking
that sets free
the commingling of sane
and insane fragments
moments when the light
burns through
to the meek
suspension of air?